BOOK ANALYSIS

Written by Elena Pinaud
Translated by Ciaran Traynor

No and Me
BY DELPHINE DE VIGAN

Bright
≡Summaries.com

DELPHINE DE VIGAN 11

French novelist

NO AND ME 15

The moving story of an unlikely friendship

SUMMARY 19

The meeting
The presentation
Lucas
No's disappearance

CHARACTER STUDY 27

Lou Bertignac
No
Lucas
Anouk Bertignac
Bernard Bertignac

ANALYSIS 35

A humanist novel
The theme of loneliness
A coming-of-age novel
Rationality versus spontaneity
Writing the world as it is

FURTHER REFLECTION 47

Some questions to think about…

FURTHER READING 51

DELPHINE DE VIGAN

FRENCH NOVELIST

- **Born in Boulogne-Billancourt (France) in 1966.**
- **Notable works:**
    - *Days Without Hunger* (2001), novel
    - *Underground Time* (2009), novel
    - *Nothing Holds Back the Night* (2011), novel

Delphine de Vigan was born in the Paris region in 1966. In 2001, she became known to the general public with her autobiographical novel on anorexia, *Days Without Hunger*, which was published under the pseudonym Lou Delvig. She then moved on to write a collection of short stories, *Les jolis garçons* ("The Pretty Boys", 2005), and a novel, *Un soir de décembre* ("One December Evening", 2005), which had love as their main theme. In 2008, she received the Prix des libraires for her bestseller *No and Me* and the Prix Renaudot young adult for *Nothing Holds Back the Night*.

In 2015, her novel *Based on a True Story* won the Prix Renaudot.

NO AND ME

THE MOVING STORY OF AN UNLIKELY FRIENDSHIP

- **Genre**: novel
- **Reference edition**: De Vigan, D. (2010) *No and Me*. Trans. Miller, G. London: Bloomsbury.
- **1st edition**: 2010
- **Themes**: friendship, mutual help, difference, poverty, homelessness

No and Me, adapted for the big screen in 2010, is the first person story of a gifted 13-year-old called Lou Bertignac. She shares her questions on life, on family and human relations, on love, and, most importantly, on human poverty with the reader. Lou meets an 18-year-old homeless girl, No, who she helps to get off the streets. A real friendship blossoms between the girls.

The story is both simple and touching. The author's main talent lies in the description of Lou's emotions, of her feelings, hopes, and disappointments, and of what she learns about life. *No and*

Me is a life lesson which combines both social and personal elements.

SUMMARY

THE MEETING

At Austerlitz railway station in Paris, a young girl named Lou Bertignac meets a young homeless girl called Nolwenn, who goes by the name of No. She immediately decides to make the homeless the subject of her social and economic sciences presentation. "I'm going to follow the journey of a homeless girl", she announces (p. 5). She still does not realise how much this meeting will change her life.

In order to prepare her presentation, the young girl invites No out for a drink to discuss her journey, but at first No would rather just listen to Lou. Over the course of their meetings, Lou learns that the young woman is 18 years old, that she has been on the street for a few months and that she is sometimes taken in by people she knows. Lou fills an entire notebook with No's account and begins to research the homeless to prepare for her presentation.

During one of their meetings, Lou notices that No is extremely beautiful in spite of her dirty hair. Once she gets home, she recalls every word of their discussion. When the family sit down to eat, her father is as animated as ever, but this time Lou does not take part in the conversation. She is very troubled by her mother's lack of interest, as she has been depressed for several years after the death of Lou's two-month-old sister, Chloe.

THE PRESENTATION

After Lou does her presentation, she is applauded by her classmates and given 18 out of 20. She then goes back to the train station to share her success with No, but the young woman is not there. The woman who works in the newspaper kiosk tells Lou that she has not been there for some time. She adds that Lou should put an end to her friendship with the homeless girl, because the two live in two completely different worlds.

Next, Lou goes to a supermarket where an old friend of No's works. She wants to find out if she has heard anything from the young woman, but No's friend knows no more than the lady in the station. Lou then goes to look for her on the street where another homeless person would sometimes take her in, and the man tells her that she might find No in one of the city's soup kitchens. He turns out to be right, and Lou finds No a few days later queueing for a ticket. However, her friend pushes her away violently "I don't need you", "Get lost, Lou, do you hear? [...] This isn't your life, do you understand? It's not your life." Lost and angry with No, Lou leaves: "I think at that moment I hate her – her and all the homeless people on Earth. All they need to do is be nicer, less dirty and they'd be fine. All they have to do is make an effort to be pleasant, instead of boozing on park benches and spitting."

LUCAS

One day, Lou is surprised to find No outside her school. She invites her to go for something to eat. No tells her that she is living in an emergency shelter and is looking for work. However, since she has no fixed address, nobody wants to hire her. Lou then tells her about her feelings for Lucas, a boy at her school.

After the holidays, Lucas sat beside her on the

school bus and asked her to go ice skating with him. Lou is excited that Lucas, who she finds incredibly good-looking, would rather spend time with her than with the other girls. She asks No how to kiss a boy, which makes the young woman laugh and make a few passing comments about her relationship with a boy named Laurent.

So that No has an address and can therefore find work, Lou has the idea of taking her in. She manages to convince her parents. At first, No sleeps a lot and often tells Lou "We're together." She gets on well with Anouk Bertignac, Lou's mother, who she confides her origins to and also helps with the housework. In the meantime, Lucas begins to invite the two girls to his house quite often and spends a lot of time at school with Lou.

No is finally hired as a cleaning lady in a hotel. The work is difficult and it takes its toll on No, who begins to be nasty to Lou. One day, she decides to go see her mother, who lives in social housing, and Lou goes with her. But when No knocks at the door, her mother refuses to open it, even when the young girl insists and grows angry.

Shortly afterwards, the Bertignacs go to Dordogne for a few days. When they return to Paris, they notice that something has changed: No, who is working the night shift, is drinking a lot, leaving things lying around everywhere and not going to her meetings with her social worker. Bernard, Lou's father, warns her that she has to follow the rules if she wants to keep living with them. As a result, No goes to stay with Lucas.

NO'S DISAPPEARANCE

Lucas and Lou decide to look after No in secret. No begins to save up to go see her friend Laurent, who is working in Ireland. But the young girl continues to drink, which causes problems for Lucas, making him late for school and stopping him from doing his homework. Furthermore, No has a lot of money and refuses to explain where she got it from.

When Lou's parents discover what their daughter has been up to, they warn Lucas' mother. No is forced to go, and Lou wants to leave everything behind to go and live with her in Ireland. While waiting for their departure, the two girls spend the day at the cinema and in cafés, and No pays for everything. In the morning, after spending the night in a rather average hotel, they go to the Gare Saint-Lazare to buy tickets for England, from where they plan to take the ferry to Ireland. No, who wants to buy the tickets herself, asks Lou to wait for her. A few hours later, she has still not returned. Lou therefore goes home and makes up with her parents. She and Lucas go to visit No's old friend who works in the supermarket, who has not heard anything from No and says that Laurent was never in a relationship with the homeless girl, in spite of what No may have claimed.

One day, Lucas unexpectedly takes Lou and kisses her.

CHARACTER STUDY

LOU BERTIGNAC

Lou is a 13-year-old girl who is very bright for her age. She has skipped two years at school, which makes her the youngest in her class. Her father encourages her to develop her intellectual curiosity by giving her encyclopaedias, which she devours. After her mother became depressed, she was placed in a school for gifted children in Nanterre and only went home every two weeks. Each time she left, she hoped that "one day he'd [her father] put his foot down on the accelerator [...] and drive all three of us into the wall of a car park, and we'd be together forever." It is at this point that her feeling of loneliness begins to grow stronger.

It is this feeling which makes her take an interest in No's fate. The young homeless girl's daily life is for Lou "a priceless gift, but one of such weight that I'm afraid I'm unworthy of it. It's a gift that changes the world's colours and calls all theories into question." Profoundly affected by how the young girl lives, Lou does everything in her power to save her. Having someone to turn to and no longer being alone "makes a difference" not only to No, but also to Lou. The young girl refuses to accept that human beings should live in different worlds separated by arbitrary criteria like money or power. She would like to be in a place "where worlds communicate with each other." By helping No and becoming her friend, she wants to bring these two universes together.

Lou does not like speaking in public, because she feels that she cannot master the power words have and prefers to keep "the extra words, the overflow [...] the words that I silently multiply to get close to the truth" to herself. Even if she is not very talkative with her classmates or her parents, her mind is always ticking. She thinks about things constantly, counts things, makes parallels and comparisons and, above all, observes. She is amazed, for example, that humans can fly into space and yet at the same time let homeless people die in the streets. She often goes to the Austerlitz railway station because it is the ideal place to observe human emotions: "You've got to work out what people are feeling from their expressions, from their gestures and movements [...] you get all sorts of people [...] – young, old, well dressed, fat, thin, scruffy. The lot" (pp. 7-8).

It is thanks to No that Lou grows as a person: she gains the strength to fight not only for those who are less fortunate than herself, but also to overcome her shyness with Lucas. Even if she fails in her mission to 'save' No, she grows in confidence and matures greatly.

NO

No is an 18-year-old girl whose real name is Nolwenn. As she grows more comfortable with Lou, we learn that she was born of rape when her mother was just 15 years old. Coming from a poor family, her mother had no other choice than to keep the baby, but hated her from the moment she was born, and found herself incapable of calling No by name, touching her or playing with her. No was therefore brought up by her grandparents, who were Breton farmers. When her grandmother died, No went back to her mother, but she continued to reject her. Her only moments of pleasure were when her step-dad would play with her and speak softly to her. However, he ended up leaving No's mother because she was jealous of her daughter. Her mother then became an alcoholic, and No was forced to stay off school to help her. Social services finally put the young girl in a foster family, where she was treated well. However, since she was a teenager who had already acquired a taste for independence and dangerous experiences (drinking alcohol, smoking cigarettes, and keeping strange company), she ran away often. She was therefore sent to boarding school where she met Laurent, who she fell in love with. At 18 years old, she found herself without any qualifications and with no one to stay with. She therefore became homeless.

When she meets Lou, she explains that the homeless people she talks to are not her friends, because "on the streets you don't have friends." "She tells me about the fear, the cold, the wandering around [and] violence", and she breaks off often to drink, smoke or just sit for a while in silence. Lou interprets this as a sign of powerlessness: "our silence is filled with all the world's impotence. Our silence is like the return to the origin of things, their true state."

Her experience of being homeless has made her unstable and sensitive: she does not think twice before rejecting Lou, even though she is her friend. It has also stripped away her sense of pride (she spits, insults people and bites her nails). When she has money, she spends it without thinking about it: she buys Lou a pair of very expensive training shoes and, the night before she is due to leave for England, she invites her friend to the cinema and pays for everything.

She seems to hold the same view of the world as the newspaper seller, since she cannot adapt to the rules of the Bertignac household. She ends up leaving her friend.

LUCAS

Lucas is a 17-year-old boy who Lou and the other students think is very handsome. He is not interested in school and is a bad student: he has already had to resit two years. He has a blasé attitude which draws girls' attention and irritates teachers.

Just like Lou and No, he is lonely: his father left the family to live in Brazil and his mother met someone else. She rarely comes to see her son. Lucas therefore has to get by on his own.

He decides to help No and supports Lou in everything she does. Lucas makes up stories about No's future ("a better future for her, lucky breaks, fairy tales") to give her courage. He is not blind to Lou's (or, as he calls her, Chip) feelings: he understands them and, above all, shares them.

ANOUK BERTIGNAC

Anouk Bertignac is Lou's mother. After the sudden death of her second child, she retreats into silence and becomes more and more distant and no longer participates in family or professional life. She ends up seriously depressed and has to be treated in a special hospital.

However, No's arrival in the household changes things: to Lou's surprise and her husband's delight, Anouk begins to change and open up to the people around her. In fact, the homeless girl manages to unearth a maternal instinct buried deep inside Mrs Bertignac. Anouk and No become friends, confiding in one another, lending each other their clothes and drinking wine together.

At the end of the book, having finished mourning her dead child, Anouk realises that she has neglected her own daughter for too long. When Lou disappears, she is extremely worried about her. Thanks to this event, Anouk grows as a person and goes back to being how she was before the death of little Chloe.

BERNARD BERTIGNAC

Unlike his wife, Bernard Bertignac hides the signs that he is depressed. As he is a manager, he does not permit himself to cry in public. In reality, he is powerless before a depressed wife and a gifted teenager.

He embodies the adult values of responsibility, stability and order. He feels that he has a civic duty to No: he clears a desk for her and calls the social worker. Even so, he is still forced to throw her out of the house when she does not respect the rules. After doing so, his relationship with Lou deteriorates, and she accuses him of not understanding anything.

ANALYSIS

A HUMANIST NOVEL

The novel is not a criticism of social class (since it does not favour any one class over the other) but rather underlines one of the issues with modern-day society: the worrying number of homeless people and the difficulties they face in trying to escape the streets. It could be better described as a humanist novel, in that it puts humanity and its values above all else.

How can people end up on the street? Lou does not understand it. For example, the homeless man who lived in their area for years found himself on the street after his wife left him, because he could not handle the situation and lost his way, both personally and socially. No gives some other examples: "normal women who've lost their jobs or run away from home. Women who've been beaten or thrown out."

Homeless people, who are already living in a very difficult situation, become even poorer in the long run. They cannot find work, they are forced to queue for a bowl of soup, they are chased out of shops as soon as they go inside to warm themselves up, and so on. Prospective employers take advantage of their weakness, as No has already experienced: she is a part-time employee who works full time and, in addition to cleaning, has to watch the bar and greet guests.

Furthermore, there is a lot of violence between the homeless, as the soup kitchen scene shows, where everyone is fighting for a place, or the scene where two women come to blows over a cigarette end. "Animals. Fucking animals" No says as she recounts this story to Lou. They seem to belong to another universe, which is exactly what No thinks. When she casually walks past a homeless person who has taken her in a few times and pretends not to see him, Lou – who is walking with her – points out that he is her friend. No, who at this point has a job, goes back to the man and gives him 20 euros, but he refuses the note and spits on the ground. Could he too be convinced that the homeless are part of another world than those who are financially stable and that, in their world, there are unspoken rules to be respected, a sort of hierarchy or a dignity which is difficult to comprehend?

Delphine de Vigan is therefore pointing out how dysfunctional our modern society is, where we are capable of making technical progress but incapable of looking out for our peers, for the destitute. Society is becoming more and more mechanised and dehumanised. This seems to be Lou's conclusion as well. The author is therefore using her novel to denounce the rejection and stigmatisation of the homeless by certain people, who treat them with total indifference.

It should also be noted that the author is trying to highlight the omnipresence of violence, which is not only evident among the homeless. Lou, who thought that violence was only ever physical, discovers the many forms it can truly take through No's silences ("There's violence in the time that conceals wounds [...] the impossibility of turning back the clock"), her mother's lack of reactions ("My mother remains standing [...] her arms dangling beside her body. There is violence there too, in that impossible gesture she makes towards me, that gesture frozen in time for eternity"[1]) and everyday life ("All you had to do was see how people looked, to count the ones who were talking to themselves or had gone off the rails – all you had to do was take the metro"). In modern society, violence is everywhere.

In spite of all that, Lou wants to prove that all you have to do is look around and open yourself to others to change the course of events.

> "One day you latch on to one of these silhouettes, to a person. You ask questions, try to find reasons and explanations. [...] Things are what they are. But I believe we've got to keep our eyes wide open."

THE THEME OF LONELINESS

Loneliness among young people is also evident in the novel.

Lou, a girl from a loving, well-off family, feels lonely (this is an expression which she repeats on several occasions) and finds a friend in the form of No, in spite of the fact that all the two have in common is their loneliness. When she decides

---

1. This quotation has been translated by BrightSummaries.com.

to help No instead of abandoning her, she is the only one to do so (her parents are happy to have No only as long as she respects their rules).

Lou is well aware of when her solitude began: one day, after the death of her sister, she fell while she was cycling in the park with her mother, but Anouk saw nothing and did not react. Another lady helped her to her feet instead, after which her mother beckoned her with a wave: "a wave like that [...] means you're going to have to be strong, you'll need lots of courage and you'll have to grow up with that. Or rather without." Without, in this case, refers to her mother's affection.

No was also abandoned by her mother and for a little while takes a certain comfort in the presence of Anouk Bertignac. Consequently, when No confides in Anouk, Lou has the impression that she is trying to find a substitute mother. The young girl grows angry, especially when she hears Anouk tell No how her baby died (she feels betrayed by her mother for a second time). But No's loneliness is a social loneliness more than anything else: there can never be any connection between her and the homeless people she associates with, and the social work system does nothing but put more pressure on her. In order to protect herself, she therefore sets up a sort of defence system against everything, which takes the form of a kind of independence, as she rejects all attempts at help or friendship (her nickname is also a nod to this). She accepts Lou and Lucas's help for a while, but eventually leaves them as well.

Lucas suffers from another form of loneliness. He is quite simply abandoned by his parents, despite the fact that they still love him and believe they can make up for their absence with money. He is strong enough to overcome his solitude and become an adult confident in his own abilities.

A COMING-OF-AGE NOVEL

No and Me is a coming-of-age novel in which Lou, a young teenager, is thrown into the reality of life and begins to gain an understanding of human relationships and how society works. She is faced with different aspects of the world (the homeless, love and lack of love, friendship) which influence her development and help her to form personal opinions.

Lou, who was always alone, discovers what friendship is and begins to view it in a very utopian manner. She thinks about the fox in *The Little Prince* by Saint-Exupéry (French writer, 1900–1944), in the part about the meaning of the verb 'to tame', which she memorised and wants to put to the test.

> "To me, you are still nothing more than a little boy who is just like a hundred thousand other little boys. And I have no need of you. And you, on your part, have no need of me. To you, I am nothing more than a fox like a hundred thousand other foxes. But if you tame me, then we shall need each other. To me, you will be unique in all the world. To you, I shall be unique in all the world . . ." (*The Little Prince*, p. 46).

She is tamed by No and consequently begins to need her friendship so as not to feel alone any more. No therefore becomes unique to Lou. But it is unclear whether No accepts being or expects to be tamed: the fact that she abandons Lou and rejects her at different points throughout the story shows that she has doubts about forging close relationships, even if she constantly reassures herself of Lou's trust in her. This is not simple indifference as Lou believes: given that No has never received much attention from her family, she does not know how to react.

Lou sees her friendship put to the test and, throughout the novel, learns much about human relationships.

RATIONALITY VERSUS SPONTANEITY

When confronted with homeless people, there are two approaches which are explored in the novel: adult rationality versus youthful spontaneity or impulsiveness.

The first approach (evident in Bernard Bertignac, the social and economic sciences teacher or even the newspaper woman) is more theoretical than practical: they simply talk, warn and look for arguments while comparing the data and statistics about homeless people. Rather cautious and passive, they see the world in black and white.

On the other hand there is Lou, and later Lucas, who both decide to go out onto the streets to discover an unknown world. The two teenagers take concrete, tangible action (for example, by feeding No and offering her a place to stay to facilitate her job hunting). Their help does not come with any strings attached. When No's alcoholism begins to become a problem, they do not throw her out, as Bernard does, but rather redouble their efforts to help her.

The difference comes down to how they look at the issue: the teenagers are more naïve, and they observe but do not judge. They also ask themselves questions which adults, like robots programmed to follow a set routine, no longer do.

WRITING THE WORLD AS IT IS

De Vigan's world is not perfect. The author does not try to preach or elicit an emotional response from the reader. The statement "things are what they are", a recurring theme in the novel, could quite easily describe the writer's style: she writes things the way they are, without frills, in order to describe reality the way that people see it.

In a certain way, the theme of homelessness serves as a pretext to tackle a subject as complex as it is universal: human relationships (for example between mother and daughter, classmates, or the people you meet in the supermarket), or even social exclusion.

Moreover, the intentionally simple (or simplified) language of the book is designed to make it understandable to young people. In order to do this, the author, herself the mother of two children, made sure to spend time and correspond with teenagers. In order to avoid any pitfalls, de Vigan lends her own voice to Lou, the gifted, lovable and genuine teenager (Eliard, 2008).

A LOOSE ADAPTATION

After showing genuine interest in the characters, director Zabou Breitman (French actress and director, born in 1959) adapted *No and Me* for the cinema in 2010. She herself played the part of Anouk Bertignac, with Bernard Campan (French actor, born in 1958) at her side in the role of Bernard Bertignac, Nina Rodriguez (French actress, born in 1997) in the role of Lou and Julie-Marie Parmentier (French actress, born in 1981) as No, who is called Nora in the film.

The film was nominated for five awards, and the award for Most Promising Actor at the Lumières Awards went to the director's son Antonin Chalon (French actor, born in 1993), who played Lucas.

In *No and Me*, the author describes the meeting of two teenagers who are from different worlds but are equally lost: there is the gifted young girl who comes from a 'normal' world and has a lot of flaws, and the young homeless girl who has already been worn out by life. Their closeness, in spite of their differences, is what allowed the novel to be so commercially successful.

FURTHER REFLECTION

SOME QUESTIONS TO THINK ABOUT…

- Which human values are displayed in this work?
- Does the author take a 'socially committed' approach? Could it be argued that she is implying that the current social system should be denounced?
- How would you explain Lou's feeling of loneliness?
- We meet three different mothers in this novel. Describe and compare them.
- Lou is intellectually advanced for her age. How does she deal with this? Does she feel that this is useful in everyday life?
- Although Lou has an IQ of 160, she finds herself at a loss in relatively simple situations. Do some research on gifted people to explain this and better understand them.
- No prefers not to talk directly about herself. Why, in your opinion?

- Imagine you have to do a presentation on the topic of homelessness. What would you say?
- *No and Me* was adapted for the big screen in 2010. Compare the impact of the film (which comes from its visual aspect) to that of the book (which comes from reading) on the public.
- This book was very successful among young people. What would you attribute this success to?

We want to hear from you!
Leave a comment on your online library
and share your favourite books on social media!

FURTHER READING

REFERENCE EDITION

- De Vigan, D. (2010) *No and Me*. Trans. Miller, G. London: Bloomsbury (Original work published 2007).

REFERENCE STUDY

- Eliard, A. (2008) Delphine de Vigan, mi-guépard mi-hérisson. *Le Figaro*. [Online]. [Accessed 1 October 2016]. Available from: <http://www.lefigaro.fr/livres/2008/07/01/03005-20080701ARTFIG00284-delphine-de-vigan-mi-guepard-mi-herisson.php>

ADDITIONAL SOURCES

- De Saint Exupéry, A. (1943) *The Little Prince*. Trans. Woods, K. San Diego: Harcourt, Brace & World.

ADAPTATION

- *No and Me*. (2010) [Film]. Zabou Breitman. Dir. France: Diaphana.

MORE FROM BRIGHTSUMMARIES.COM

- Reading guide – *Based on a True Story* by Delphine de Vigan.
- Reading guide – *Nothing Holds Back the Night* by Delphine de Vigan.
- Reading guide – *Underground Time* by Delphine de Vigan.

Bright ≡Summaries.com

More guides to rediscover your love of literature

Animal Farm BY GEORGE ORWELL

The Stranger BY ALBERT CAMUS

Harry Potter and the Sorcerer's Stone BY J.K. ROWLING

The Silence of the Sea BY VERCORS

Antigone BY JEAN ANOUILH

The Flowers of Evil BY BAUDELAIRE

www.brightsummaries.com

Although the editor makes every effort to verify the accuracy of the information published, BrightSummaries.com accepts no responsibility for the content of this book.

© BrightSummaries.com, 2016. All rights reserved.

www.brightsummaries.com

Ebook EAN: 9782806294425

Paperback EAN: 9782806294418

Legal Deposit: D/2017/12603/109

This guide was written with the collaboration of Tina Van Roeyen on the characters of Anouk Bertignac and Bernard Bertignac, and also for the sections 'Rationality versus spontaneity' and 'Writing the world as it is'.

Cover: © Primento

Digital conception by Primento, the digital partner of publishers.

Printed in Great Britain
by Amazon